CANCER

—SUN SIGN SERIES—

CANCER

SUN SIGN SERIES
JOANNA MARTINE WOOLFOLK

TAYLOR TRADE PUBLISHING
LANHAM • NEW YORK • BOULDER • TORONTO • PLYMOUTH, UK

Published by Taylor Trade Publishing

An imprint of The Rowman & Littlefield Publishing Group, Inc.

4501 Forbes Boulevard, Suite 200, Lanham, Maryland 20706

www.rlpgtrade.com

Estover Road, Plymouth PL6 7PY, United Kingdom

Distributed by National Book Network

· British Library Cataloguing in Publication Information Available

Library of Congress Cataloging-in-Publication Data

Woolfolk, Joanna Martine.
 Cancer / Joanna Martine Woolfolk.
  p. cm.—(Sun sign series)
 ISBN 978-1-58979-556-3 (pbk. : alk. paper)—ISBN 978-1-58979-531-0 (electronic)
 1. Cancer (Astrology) I. Title.
 BF1727.3.W66 2011
 133.5'265—dc22   2011003079

∞^{TM} The paper used in this publication meets the minimum requirements of American National Standard for Information Sciences—Permanence of Paper for Printed Library Materials, ANSI/NISO Z39.48-1992.

Printed in the United States of America

I dedicate this book to the memory of
William Woolfolk
whose wisdom continues to guide me,

and to
James Sgandurra
who made everything bloom again.

CONTENTS

ABOUT THE AUTHOR

Astrologer Joanna Martine Woolfolk has had a long career as an author, columnist, lecturer, and counselor. She has written the monthly horoscope for numerous magazines in the United States, Europe, and Latin America—among them *Marie Claire*, *Harper's Bazaar*, *Redbook*, *Self*, *YM*, *House Beautiful*, and *StarScroll International*. In addition to the best-selling *The Only Astrology Book You'll Ever Need*, Joanna is the author of *Sexual Astrology*, which has sold over a million copies worldwide, and *Astrology Source*, an interactive CD-ROM.

Joanna is a popular television and radio personality who has been interviewed by Barbara Walters, Regis Philbin, and Sally Jessy Raphael. She has appeared in a regular astrology segment on *New York Today* on NBC-TV and on *The Fairfield Exchange* on

CT Cable Channel 12, and she appears frequently on television and radio shows around the country. You can visit her website at www.joannamartinewoolfolk.com.

ACKNOWLEDGMENTS

Many people contribute to the creation of a book, some with ideas and editorial suggestions, and some unknowingly through their caring and love.

Among those who must know how much they helped is Jed Lyons, the elegant, erudite president of my publishers, the Rowman & Littlefield Publishing Group. Jed gave me the idea for this Sun Sign series, and I am grateful for his faith and encouragement.

Enormous gratitude also to Michael K. Dorr, my literary agent and dear friend, who has believed in me since we first met and continues to be my champion. I thank Michael for his sharp editor's eye and imbuing me with confidence.

Two people who don't know how much they give are my beloved sister and brother, Patricia G. Reynhout and Dr. John T. Galdamez. They sustain me with their unfailing devotion and support.

*We are born at a given moment, in a given place,
and like vintage years of wine, we have the
qualities of the year and of the season
in which we are born.*

Carl Gustav Jung

INTRODUCTION

When my publishers suggested I write a book devoted solely to Cancer, I was thrilled. I've long wanted to concentrate exclusively on your wonderful sign. You are very special in the zodiac. Astrology teaches that Cancer is the sign of creative force and emotional power. Your sign represents the concept of giving birth—to ideas, artistic expression, relationships, and human life. You have ambition, imagination, tenacity, and devotion. Especially, you're know for your qualities of protectiveness (looking after people and projects) and your intensely loving heart. Karmic teachers say you were specially picked to be a Cancer because of the nurturing, caring, and even sacrifice you gave in your previous life. But whether or not one believes in past lives, in *this* life you are Cancer, the great artist and creator of something that lasts.

These days it has become fashionable to be a bit dismissive of Sun signs (the sign that the Sun was in at the time of your birth). Some people sniff that "everyone knows about Sun signs." They say the descriptions are too "cookie-cutter," too much like cardboard figures, too inclusive (how can every Cancer be the same?).

Of course every Cancer is not the same! And many of these differences are not only genetic and environmental, but differences in your *charts*. Another Cancerian would not necessarily have your Moon sign, or Venus sign, or Ascendant. However, these are factors to consider later—after you have studied your Sun sign. (In *The Only Astrology Book You'll Ever Need*, I cover in depth differences in charts: different Planets, Houses, Ascendants, etc.)

First and foremost, you are a Cancer. This is the sign the Sun was traveling through at the time of your birth.* The Sun is our most powerful planet. (In astrological terms, the Sun is referred to as a planet even though technically it is a "luminary.") It gives us life, warmth, energy, and food. It is the force that sustains us on Earth. The Sun is also the most important and pervasive influence in your horoscope and in many ways determines how others see you. Your Sun sign governs your individuality, your distinctive style, and your drive to fulfill your goals.

Your sign of Cancer symbolizes the role you are given to play in this life. It's as if at the moment of your birth you were pushed onstage into a drama called *This Is My Life*. In this drama, you are the starring actor—and Cancer is the character you play. What aspects of this character are you going to project? The Cancer creativity and imagination? Its compassion, sensitivity, and warmhearted empathy for others? Or its possessiveness and crabbiness? Your sign of Cancer describes your journey through this life, for it is your task to evolve into a perfect Cancer.

For each of us, the most interesting, most gripping subject is *self*. The longer I am an astrologer—which at this point is half my lifetime—the more I realize that what we all want to know about is ourselves. "Who am I?" you ask. You want to know what makes you tick, why you have such intense feelings, and whether others

---

*From our viewpoint here on Earth, the Sun travels around the Earth once each year. Within the space of that year the Sun moves through all twelve signs of the zodiac, spending approximately one month in each sign.

are also insecure. People ask me questions like "What kind of man should I look for?" "Why am I discontented with my job?" or "The woman I'm dating is a Scorpio; will we be happy together?" They ask me if they'll ever find true love and when they will get out of a period of sadness or fear or the heavy burden of problems. They ask about their path in life and how they can find more fulfillment.

So I continue to see that the reason astrology exists is to answer questions about you. Basically, it's all about *you*. Astrology has been described as a stairway leading into your deeper self. It holds out the promise that you do not have to pass through life reacting blindly to experience, that you can, within limits, direct your own destiny and in the process reach a truer self-understanding.

Astrologically, the place to begin the study of yourself is your Sun sign. In this book, you'll read about your many positive qualities as well as your Cancer issues and negative inclinations. You'll find insights into your power and potentials, advice about love and sex, career guidance, health and diet tips, and information about myriads of objects, places, concepts, and things to which Cancer is attached. You'll also find topics not usually included in other astrology books—such as how Cancer fits in with Chinese astrology and with numerology.

Come with me on this exploration of the "infinite variety" (in Shakespeare's phrase) of being a Cancer.

Joanna Martine Woolfolk
Stamford, Connecticut
June 2011

CANCER
JUNE 21–JULY 22

Pl. 19

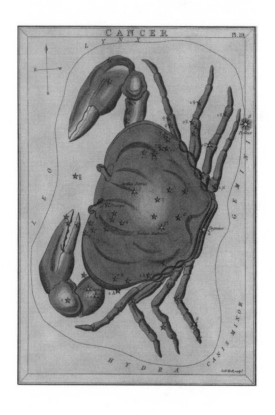

PART ONE

ALL ABOUT YOU

ILLUMINATING QUOTATIONS

"It is only with the heart that one can see rightly. What is essential is invisible to the eye."

—Antoine de Saint-Exupery, novelist, a Cancerian

"The biggest disease the world suffers from is the disease of people feeling unloved."

—Diana, Princess of Wales, a Cancerian

"What is moral is what you feel good after, and what is immoral is what you feel bad after."

—Ernest Hemingway, author, a Cancerian

"You're only given a little spark of madness. You mustn't lose it."

—Robin Williams, actor and comedian, a Cancerian

"Winners are the ones who really listen to the truth of their hearts."

—Sylvester Stallone, actor and writer, a Cancerian

"Everything we do in life is based on fear, especially love."

—Mel Brooks, writer, director, and comedian, a Cancerian

YOUR CANCER PERSONALITY

YOUR MOST LIKEABLE TRAIT: Loyalty

The bright side of Cancer: Imaginative, nurturing, giving, patient
The dark side of Cancer: Possessive, a worrier, irritable, critical, self-pitying

Cancer represents foundation, home, family, and security. It is the sign linked to the concept of giving birth—to ideas, artistic expression, relationships, and to human life. You have a deeply sensitive and caring nature and tend to be tenacious, protective, and often overpossessive. When you devote yourself, whether to a person or a project, you focus on the well-being of that entity. Being a Water sign, you're emotional and subject to mood swings. You make decisions from the heart, not the head, and are most comfortable in the realm of imagination and intuition. Cancer is also a Cardinal sign, which means you enjoy initiating projects. You gravitate to creative work that expresses feelings and creates bonds with people. Love brings out the best in you, for you are deeply loyal as well as passionate. You flourish in committed relationships.

No one ever said you're easy to understand. You may seem gentle, kind, and sympathetic, and appear to be a patient listener. Then someone asks for advice, and you turn cranky and snappish and appear to be completely indifferent to anyone's problems but your own. You may wallow in self-pity and complain endlessly about how mistreated you are by the world. Turn another page of the calendar, and suddenly you are back to being helpful and solicitous, ready to do anything asked of you. More than any other sign, Cancer is a series of contradictions. You prize security above all else, yet love new adventure. You are the soul of caution, but you're also a courageous initiator who goes out of your way to push over obstacles with your driving personality.

What's your secret? Cancer, which is ruled by the waxing and waning Moon and has water as its element, can be likened to the shifting tides of the oceans. Like the tides, Cancer is the sign of powerful forces moving under the surface. That surface, however, is quite difficult to penetrate, for Cancerians tend to build up an elaborate array of defenses to hide their deep feelings and extreme sensitivity.

Complex, fragile, unpredictable, temperamental, the typical Cancerian needs constant support and encouragement. You want desperately to be loved and approved of, but resent needing approval so badly. Cancer's big lesson is to recognize the hidden anger you carry within you and not allow this to corrode the relationships that give you the emotional support you seek. Happily, when you get what you need, you give the best you have in return. Those who make you feel secure command your undying loyalty. When you really care for someone, there is nothing anyone can say about that person that will make the least bit of difference. You have a real blind spot when it comes to seeing a failing in those you love.

If you could wave a magic wand and do the one thing that would make you happier, it would be to crack open that crab shell around you and venture out into the world of possibility. Staying enclosed emotionally and psychically keeps you fearful. Cancer's fears are based on the fact that you have a difficult time trusting. You don't trust others or the universe or yourself. One Cancer told me recently, "We've been sold a bill of goods by the stories we were told as children. There is no joy or happiness in life. Life is just plain hard." The problem with this point of view is it leaves very little opening for any kind of abundance to flow in. It's hard to see the kindness in loved ones or the generosity of strangers or unexpected luck in an arduous situation if one has decided from the start that it's a dog-eat-dog world.

Yet most contradictory of all is the fact that you're such a nurturer who gives unselfishly to anyone who needs you. Your greatest impact is in human relationships; you have an instinct for making others feel cared for and understood. Among your most endearing traits is your fidelity.

You tend to be a worrier and a silent brooder. People may pour out their hearts to you, but the flow never goes in the other direction. You are cautious about revealing too much of yourself; you guard your secrets well.

If offended, you do not strike back directly. Being a passive-aggressor, your method of retaliation is to sulk, and it is often very effective. The technique is somewhat like being whipped to death by a dozen strands of boiled spaghetti.

Cancer's symbol, the Crab, has a hard outer shell that protects soft, vulnerable flesh underneath. The same is true of Cancerians, who are often crusty, gruff, and grumpy, but who possess a proverbial heart of gold. Beneath your tough exterior you are a sentimental softie who will make any sacrifice for someone in need. If someone asks for a favor, your first reaction will probably be no, but the final answer is always yes. You should be judged not by what you say but by what you do—you show your caring in deeds.

Cancer is the cosmic collector. In every area (relationships, money, career), you try to hold on to what you have and store up more. You are possessive. Anyone who becomes part of your life will never again be entirely free. You stay in touch with friends, ex-lovers, former spouses, business associates, persons you knew as children. If you let anyone go out of your life, it is unwillingly and never completely. This reflects your preoccupation with the past. An aura of nostalgia dwells about you; the events and people of bygone years continue to inhabit your memory and usually grow dearer to you as time goes by. You are devoted to family and home—your fixed point is always your home, which you retreat to in times of stress. You continue to believe in the old-fashioned idea that marriage is forever, even if the events of your own life contradict this.

It is hard to deceive you, for you can spot the tiniest nuances of behavior. You see what lies beneath the surface. In fact, you are almost psychic in your intuitions. A photographic memory added to intense powers of observation makes you keenly astute about divining people's inner motivations—and others find your insights and perceptions uncanny.

Cancerians are crablike in their indirect approach to an intended target. Observe a crab moving on a beach, and you will notice its strange sidewise movement toward a goal. People born under the sign of the Crab never take the direct approach. You don't confront—you're a master at indirection. In your life, as opposed to mathematics, the shortest distance between two points is not necessarily a straight line. You step to one side, then step to the other side, and sometimes go completely around. But you get where you intend to go. And you move in as quickly as a crab scuttling toward its prey when the occasion demands. You're a Cardinal sign, Cancer, which means you have the drive to get to your goal.

With you, everything springs from feelings. If you're not *emotionally* connected to a person or a project or a place, you're not really involved at all. Therefore, if channeled in the right direction, your enormous sensitivity is a great source of power. Once you overcome your shyness and touchiness and master your turbulent emotions, your intellect and imagination enable you to become a success in almost anything you undertake. In creative work, you store away mental images and information until the time comes when you can use them. You have the ability to dig into your own inner life and turn fantasy into practical ideas.

Contrary to the impression you tend to give, you can be extremely shrewd and canny in business. Cautious and conservative in your approach, you possess an antenna that quickly gauges public taste and opinion and senses new trends in the making. You're also an on-the-mark judge of people. You are artistic and creative, and have formidable intellectual talents. This instinct for business combined with imagination is magical for acquiring financial security, and Cancer is called a "money sign" because of its ability to attract wealth.

Cancer people hold on to money as tenaciously as they do to everything that belongs to them. To you money spells security, yet no matter how much wealth you accumulate you never feel really secure. That is true of your emotional security also. A Cancerian never gets enough love and approval; you always need more. It is very easy to fall in love with you—a loyal, devoted, affectionate, and protective Moon-child.

THE INNER YOU

On the surface you're the picture of calm, but underneath you tend to feel insecure and inadequate. You are positive that other people know what they're doing while you're just winging it. You also imagine the worst outcome to a scenario, never the best. You are a very emotional person; you are constantly *feeling*. Hearing a song on the radio makes you feel sentimental, and a particular scent, flower, or picture can jar your memory. You are also extraordinarily in sync with other people's feelings. In fact, you get almost as involved in your friends' problems as you do in your own. When you're close to someone, you believe you are supposed to help that person. Harmony is important to you—any kind of conflict or quarrel leaves you feeling depressed. However, you're definitely not wishy-washy; you have the courage of your convictions and the strength to stick up for what you think is right. You don't welcome change, and are hesitant about going ahead with something untried, yet this doesn't stop you from doing what has to be done.

HOW OTHERS SEE YOU

Those in your circle think of you as a "den mother"—the one who tries to fix other people's problems and make sure everyone is happy. They like your concern for their well-being and cherish your wise counsel. By why, even if they follow your advice, do they keep it a secret from you? Because they think you're controlling and don't want to be a puppet on your string. They also think you're moody. One minute you seem to care about them and the next you're crabby and to be avoided at all costs. In your career, you're viewed as someone who can quickly spot an opportunity for financial gain.

GUARD AGAINST: Hanging On Too Long

Your tenacity is one of your most positive attributes. You don't let go of the dream—you'll keep driving toward your goal even if, like the Crab, you have to move sideways toward it. Once a thing (a relationship, piece of work, idea, desire) is in your possession, you won't release it. Crabs will risk losing a claw rather than let go of their prey. But when you don't differentiate between what's healthy to keep and best left behind, problems arise. If you're living in the past, mourning over a failed relationship, holding on to old pain and anger, or refusing to abandon an unfeasible career arrangement, you are imprisoning yourself with ever-heavier burdens. Learn to release the toxic and unworkable, and then you can determinably focus on what truly brings you joy.

YOUR GREATEST CHALLENGE: Learning to Channel Your Emotional Power

Your strength lies in your capacity for feeling. You're comfortable in the waters of emotion. Yet you must be careful not to drown in those fluctuating tides. You're able to pick up on others' thoughts and moods, and especially what they're feeling toward *you*. You're easily wounded and often touchy, and you have a tendency to hold on to resentment. Be careful not to live your life controlled by your moods—an emotionally exhausting state of being. You're wonderful at relationships; at your best you offer trust, affection, and enthusiasm. When it comes to creative work, you're non-pareil. You have a gift for touching the hearts of the public and finding the lucrative path (double power). The key, Cancer, is to get out of *yourself* and turn your emotional force into the things that matter.

YOUR ALTER EGO

Astrology gives us many tools in our lives to help manage our struggles and solve problems. One of these tools is to reach into your opposite sign in the zodiac—your polarity.

For you, Cancer, this is Capricorn, sign of worldly success and achievement in the public eye. Whereas Cancer tends to be intro-spective and dwell in the interior, Capricorn looks outward. Capricorn deals with what is. It is serious, organized, and disciplined, and its point of view is pragmatic. Essentially, Capricorn energy goes into making a situation work. An idea never stays at the thinking stage—*tangible* results are what count. Capricorn barrels on to completion. Certainly, the push toward a goal is something Cancer and Capricorn have in common; both signs have this drive, and both signs seek financial security. But you, Cancer, are looking to create a nest of safety, whereas Capricorn wants to win success in the larger world. Capricorn doesn't get lost in sticky morasses or hang on to people who cause grief. It can coldly cut away from messy emotions and concentrate on what is productive.

Cancer, these are all qualities that can help you clear your mind when you're pulled and hauled by conflicted feelings. You care (perhaps too much) about what others need and want from you. You can go astray trying to deal with various possibilities and agendas. You can get lost struggling to make the right decision. And very often guilt just sucks you into situations you can't find any way out of.

But if you tap into the Capricorn "ruthlessness" and focus on action, you can spare yourself the grief and inner suffering you put yourself through. Capricorn tends to operate less from a personal standpoint and more from a position, for example, behind a desk, a title, a level of authority. This is not to say Capricorns are not caring individuals (they are!), nor that you should lose any of your immense warmth. However, if you can detach somewhat from the highly personal intensity you have about everything, the extreme up-and-down trajectories on your emotional radar-screen will calm considerably.

A psychological trick to borrow from Capricorn is to create a "self"—someone who exists alongside your real inner self. This may be just a caricature of who you are, but if you believe in that photograph (someone powerfully talented, for example, or looked up to by super-performers in your field), you can get much freer of the confusing tentacles around you. Look at a toxic situation you may be in through the realistic eyes of Capricorn. When you're being pulled down by someone else, it's a matter of survival. You have to save yourself.

In turn Capricorn has many lessons to learn from you—and among the most priceless is your emotional wisdom. This encompasses your extraordinary ability to love deeply, your understanding of all things human, and your capacity for holding relationships together. You never stint on the care and nurturing you give to others. Capricorn, too, needs to find its playful side as well as deeper tenderness by reaching into Cancer. And surely Capricorn can use your openness to innovative thought and your trust in intuitive flashes of knowledge.

CANCER IN LOVE

Secretly you long for magic, yearn for a soulmate. From the time you were young, you pictured being swept away into a passionate romance. Indeed, love is your great energy source, your dynamic life-force. However, there's an enormous contrast between your soft, sentimental, sensitive inner self and your somewhat aloof and impenetrable outer self. The vibes you convey are mixed—they say, "Come close, go away, no, come close." On first meeting you, a prospective partner sees you as charming, humorous, even flirtatious, and then—bang!—he or she runs into that indefinable chilly quality. It isn't easy to decipher you.

The answer, of course, is you know you're vulnerable and so you're careful and cautious. As much as you crave love, you cannot bear rejection. If you're a Cancer woman, you send an unspoken signal and then wait to see if the man has antennae finely tuned enough to pick it up. If you're a Cancer man, you'll play the charming courtier, the one who keeps the conversation and champagne flowing, but you don't make a direct overture. At most, you'll make an oblique suggestion that could as easily be taken for a mere risqué quip.

As with all Water signs (Cancer, Scorpio, Pisces), casual is not a word that exists in your emotional vocabulary. You seek permanence and, most of all, emotional security. When you date you're looking for long-term commitment, not just a good time. Yet because it's all-important to be able to put your trust in your lover, you proceed slowly. At a snail's pace you move deeper into a relationship, making sure at every turn that you are safe. To give your heart to someone's keeping is one of your most momentous decisions, for a betrayal is devastating. It takes a long, long time for you to forgive. In truth, you never forgive—rationally, yes, perhaps, but emotionally, never.

When you do fall in love, your whole world lights up. Love brings out the best in you; you're a passionate person who gives totally. In certain ways, your romantic journey can be likened to the story of the Sleeping Beauty—it takes love to awaken your eroticism. You have a wild libido and are full of delightful surprises. You're abundantly affectionate, very turned on by oral sex, and willing to experiment in all kinds of exotic love games. What makes you a superb lover is that you're a psychic sponge, soaking up the emotions, feelings, and desires of your partner. For you, the best part of passion is the ecstasy you feel upon surrendering totally to lust. You can easily become a love slave.

Much of your charm as a romantic companion is that you're a confirmed sentimentalist. You love to collect mementos of your relationship (e.g., ticket stubs or postcards from trips you've taken together). You frame photographs and keep your love letters. You remember magic moments—the wisp of a remembered fragrance or the sound of a foghorn across the water will evoke a tender nostalgia.

The bedrock of your personality is your sense of commitment. You invest every part of yourself in the person you love. You offer all your sympathy and intuitive understanding, and are loyal down to the wire. Given half a chance, you'll spoil your lover outrageously. And through whatever vicissitudes come your way, you stand by your mate. You have a blind spot when it comes to seeing faults in one you care for.

The problem with this is you have a very hard time letting go of a relationship, even if it turns hurtful. Rather than face the fearful unknown, you'll stay with what you know, holding on as tenaciously as if you had pincers instead of arms. You'll keep yourself imprisoned in emotional suffering.

Another pitfall in your relationships is that your caring and nurturing can easily slip into creating a claustrophobic atmosphere. You have a tendency to curb the independence of your mate. Time and again, lovers can't cope with your confining overprotectiveness and find ways to get away.

Jealousy, too, is a major problem. You must know that your chosen mate is faithful at all times—and anything that keeps you anxious and in doubt soon becomes unbearable. Your imagination can run away with you and work up whole suspicious scenarios with very little raw material. You keep asking a lover for proofs of loyalty, and the more you cling the more he or she struggles to put space between you.

As for what you need in love: security, of course, but as important is someone who can "hear" you. You need to have your feelings respected and be understood. Don't fall into the trap of giving your love just so you can be loved. Someone who ignores the creative, emotional, poetic part of you isn't worthy of you. At the very beginning of a relationship, you have wonderful instincts—and then too often you'll ignore them, thinking you can change someone. *You cannot change anyone except yourself.* Don't fall into sexual passion without being totally clear who the other person is.

Basically, your issues in love are the same as in the rest of your life—trust and control. Psychologically, you operate from the premise that if you do not trust and if you control the other person, you will not suffer loss or abandonment. This, of course, is totally illogical since no one can stave off the inevitable hurts and struggles that life will bring.

When you are able to think with your head and love with your heart, to be in the balance, you begin to unlock the prison of your fears. In a setting in which love can truly bloom, your romantic partner cannot help but recognize what an extraordinary treasure you are. You bring passion, affection, creativity, and commitment to the relationship. In a world in which so much is transitory, you are a Person for All Seasons.

TIPS FOR THOSE WHO WANT TO ATTRACT CANCER

Cancerians are vulnerable—to praise as well as criticism. Let them know directly and forthrightly how much you admire them. Nothing will draw Cancerians out of their shells more readily than the warmth of approval. Pick out a quality that you can, in all sincerity, compliment Cancer on. Do you like what he's wearing? Her smile? That ability to listen attentively? (No one is better at this than Cancer.) Say so. Don't be insincere and single out some quality merely for the sake of having something complimentary to say. Cancerians can always spot the difference between the compliment that is sincere and the one meant only to cajole.

Show Cancerians the softer side of your nature. Are you interested in charities? Talk about that. Or children? By all means. Or discuss a genuine personal problem that's troubling you. Then Cancerians will be able to show *their* best side: their empathy and ability to give constructive advice. Finances, politics, and sports are other areas that interest them greatly.

For a date, get tickets to the theater or to some art or cultural event. Cancerians respond to romantic, strongly melodic music, and are inclined to enjoy concerts and opera. A nice touch would be to pick a restaurant where there are strolling musicians.

Cancerians don't rush headlong into anything. They are essentially cautious, not to say skittish, about making a commitment. They try to avoid giving a definite yes or no. Tip: The longer they delay, the less likely that there will be a favorable outcome.

A true Cancerian sooner or later finds some cause for feeling injured. Their amazing memory dwells on the past and constantly recalls old wounds. A Cancerian who forgives and forgets is as rare as a vegetarian snake.

CANCER'S EROGENOUS ZONES: Tips for Those with a Cancer Lover

Our bodies are very sensitive to the touch of another human being. The special language of touching is understood on a level more basic than speech. Each sign is linked to certain zones and areas of the body that are especially receptive and can receive sexual messages through touch. Many books and manuals have been written about lovemaking, but few pay attention to the unique knowledge of erogenous zones supplied by astrology. You can use astrology to become a better, more sensitive lover.

For Cancer, the breasts are the key erogenous zone. Certainly for most people, the breasts are an especially sensitive area in lovemaking, but this is overridingly true for Cancerians. Both men and women born under this sign respond quickly to oral and manual manipulation of the nipples. Soft caresses, gentle bites, and kisses on this area heighten Cancer's sensuality. Run your hands over the hairs on a Cancer man's chest, just barely touching them, and you will ignite his passions. A Cancer woman derives pleasure from having her breasts touched and kissed by a lover.

To massage the breast and chest area erotically, begin by placing two fingers on Cancer's clavicle (the bone that juts out at the bottom of the neck). Using featherlight pressure, gently vibrate the flesh of each breast. Then stroke each nipple with the tip of one finger. Using your finger pad, gently stroke the pink area around the nipple (the areola). Finally, stroke each breast with your fingernails, just barely making contact with the flesh.

This massage technique will create urgent sensations of sexual desire in any Cancer woman or man.

CANCER'S AMOROUS COMBINATIONS: YOUR LOVE PARTNERS

CANCER AND ARIES

Both Cancer and Aries are sensually imaginative Cardinal signs—and you two start out like a house on fire. But it won't take long for the fire to burn out. Aries's venturesome spirit and wandering eye are certain to inflame your Cancerian jealousy. And you're easily hurt by Aries's sharp tongue. Aries's aggressive sexuality is not really your thing; you crave affection, cuddles, and lots of romance. Your essential natures clash. You like security, comfort, and domesticity; Aries needs freedom to explore new worlds. Aries is never satisfied, which keeps you in a state of anxiety that you're failing Aries's expectations. Also, the Cancer instinct is to cherish and protect a lover, an attitude that Aries finds too claustrophobic. You both like money, but Aries wants to spend it and you want to keep it. Too many temperamental problems here.

CANCER AND TAURUS

This union is a lovely mix of desire, emotional replenishing, and support. You both need security and a sense of permanence—and both of you are loving, affectionate, and passionate as well. Sexually, you're in tune, and you, Cancer, add a dash of imagination to Taurus's otherwise staid approach to lovemaking. Taurus is possessive, and that's just fine with you. You love a close, downy-nest kind of relationship. Each of you likes beautiful things, so your home and entertaining will be elegant, and together you enjoy a social life that revolves around good friends. Happily, both of you are acquisitive moneymakers, which should underwrite your joint fondness for a comfortable lifestyle. Taurus likes being catered to, and you're the one to do it. Steady-going Taurus is also good for your moodiness. What each of you needs, the other supplies.

CANCER AND GEMINI

Gemini is immediately seized by your imagination and sensuality, and you're intrigued by Gemini's wit and sparkle. But you won't find security with fickle, fly-by-night Gemini. Basically, Cancer's nature is emotional and Gemini's is cerebral, and this makes it difficult for you two to understand each other. Early on, the sexuality you ignite in each other keeps you mesmerized, but shortly you find it impossible to adjust to Gemini's playful, nonchalant attitude toward love. As a Cancer, you insist on being your lover's one and only, and you are possessive. You'll try to keep Gemini hemmed in, which Gemini can't abide. Gemini hates being swamped in sentimentality and longs for wider spaces. You two disagree on most things—how to spend your money, what friends to have, what kinds of parties to attend, where to go on a trip. It's a short countdown to the finish.

CANCER AND CANCER

You have a lot in common, and that's the trouble. Each understands the other perfectly, and you can wound each other without even trying. Two Cancers together are too sensitive, too demanding, too dependent. The Cancerian nature is to be obsessively concerned with its emotional psyche: Each of you needs an enormous amount of attention, coddling, and reassurance, and resents the other for not giving enough. A downbeat trait you share is a tendency to make the other feel like a scolded child. Oddly, even though you both dwell in feelings, two Cancers find it difficult to express feelings to each other. You want the other to sense your emotions and fill your needs. On the plus side, you have great *sexual* communication. You are sensual bedmates whose erotic imaginations are sparked by each other. But that's rarely enough. This treadmill goes nowhere.

CANCER AND LEO

It takes time for you to get used to Leo's extroverted exuberance. But otherwise generous, openhearted, strong Leo is just what you're looking for. You want a lover who can bring romantic excitement and punctuate your life with magical memories. Leo provides the *brio*, and you supply the emotional intensity. True, Leo needs to be stroked the right way, but your marvelous intuitions tell you exactly how to handle proud and flamboyant Leo. Admiration and a lot of flattery are what are needed to keep Leo purring with contentment. Both of you value high performance in career and earning money, important glue in your relationship. In the bedroom, Leo is domineering and perhaps a little too forthright sexually for you, but you can work out these differences in your lovemaking styles. And Leo's sunny disposition is a wonderful antidote for the Cancer blues that regularly descend on you.

CANCER AND VIRGO

Your responses are emotive and Virgo's are analytical, but your personalities mesh so well that it doesn't seem to matter. This can turn into a secure, comfortable, for-the-long-haul relationship. You may have to warm Virgo up a little, but there is fire under the ice, and your sweet Cancerian eroticism brings Virgo's buried passions to the surface. Granted, you both are worriers, but this tendency can be offset by you exercising caution in decision making and Virgo being practical. Certainly, each of you wants to create a secure life. The Cancer focus on financial gain works perfectly with goal-oriented Virgo. You understand Virgo's fussy ways, and steady Virgo helps balance your variable mood swings. You also display an affectionate dependency that neatly complements Virgo's need to protect. Each of you is eager to please the other. Good auguries.

CANCER AND LIBRA

As a pair, you're discordant and operate on entirely different levels. Cancer wants love to be emotionally transcendent while Libra seeks perfect intellectual communion. At first, Libra is enchanted by the romantic attention you turn on so completely, but in short order Libra steps back. Airy Libra finds you too possessive, demanding, and temperamental, and has no sympathy for your changeable disposition. Naturally, Libra's detachment makes you insecure, Libra's shallow emotions exasperate you, and Libra's indifference depresses you. Sexually, you two have a hard time establishing real rapport. You want deeply felt eroticism, but mainly Libra is turned on by fantasy. You both love a beautiful home, but Libra also needs parties and people and outside pleasures. When you turn critical, especially about Libra's extravagance, Libra starts looking elsewhere.

CANCER AND SCORPIO

Both of you are Water signs, and the splendor of this relationship lies in the profound feelings and intensity you share. Your eroticism is ignited by Scorpio's dynamic passions and preoccupation with sex, which liberates you to communicate your hidden desires. Both of you are extremely intuitive and can sense what will please the other. Because you're loyal, Scorpio's jealousy isn't provoked. Indeed, your possessiveness will actually make Scorpio feel secure. Scorpio is a fixed, tightly controlled sign, which gives you stability; you admire Scorpio's strength. In general, Scorpio is the controller here, but that's fine with you because you want the same things.

Family is important, and each is committed to love, work, and creating a haven. Together you can build a happy cocoon where you feel safe and loved. This just gets better all the time.

CANCER AND SAGITTARIUS

Your common ground is your exchange of ideas. Both of you are inquisitive and intelligent, and outgoing Sagittarius can open intellectual vistas for your imagination. Unfortunately, Sagittarius can't give you much else—certainly not the security in love you always need. At first you're a great sexual draw for curious Sagittarius, who's intrigued by your sensual intensity. But you're looking for emotional warmth, not just erotic play. Almost overnight, your jealousy is aroused by Sagittarius's flighty, faithless ways, and Sagittarius is bored by Cancer dependency. Sagittarius, who thrives on constant activity, likes to wander, while you're a stay-at-home. Your commitment to total togetherness only makes Sagittarius desperate to get away. In addition, outspoken Sagittarius's bluntness continually wounds you. Better friends than lovers.

CANCER AND CAPRICORN

Cancer and Capricorn are opposites in the zodiac, and like magnets you two instantly attract each other. Primarily, there's sexual combustion because you tap into Capricorn's earthy eroticism. Also, your goals in life are similar; you both have initiative and admire traditional values. If the two of you can overcome your opposites in temperament, you can make a winning combination. But career- and success-oriented Capricorn has too many other interests to give you all the emotional attention you need. You're romantic, sensitive, and need affection, while Capricorn is brusque, aloof, and domineering. You take Capricorn's reserve as a personal rebuff, which makes Capricorn turn more cold and judgmental. You find this painful to live with and become moody and critical. The differences may prove too great for long-term happiness.

CANCER AND AQUARIUS

Aquarius is curious and Cancer creative—and what passes at first for sexual passion is really passion of the mind. You stimulate each other because of the way you think; you find each other's interests *interesting*. However, Cancer has a warm, responsive, romantic nature that's chilled by Aquarius's cool self-possession. In turn, your physical demonstrativeness—which can indeed turn clinging—makes Aquarius feel hemmed in. Aquarius is quick-minded and unpredictable and apt to be impatient with you who are far more cautious and consider your actions carefully. And you're emotionally sensitive (Aquarius would say thin-skinned) and easily hurt by Aquarius's caustic humor. You don't understand Aquarius's essential detachment. You need to feel close and secure; Aquarius is a lone wolf. Sex may be all right, but there's little else going for you.

CANCER AND PISCES

Two Water signs together make an affectionate, sensitive couple who bolster each other's egos. Pisces is an imaginative dreamer, but you're an imaginative worker—together you can make your dreams a reality. Pisces provides romance in your life, and you are the all-protective lover Pisces needs. Both of you are emotional, intensely devoted, attuned to each other's moods. There's no one like a Cancer for understanding Pisces's hidden insecurities. Happily, the two of you share a tendency to retreat into your safe nest when the world starts crowding in. For sure you'll hit it off in the boudoir, for both of you are responsive sexually. Cancer has to take the lead, but Pisces is a very willing, erotic follower. Pisces has a superb gift for catering to your sexy whims and acting out your fantasies. A harmonious match.

YOUR CANCER CAREER PATH

The key to a career that makes you happy—and therefore brings success—is to feel at *home* with it. You must truly like what you're doing and be able to express yourself (your opinions, ideas, taste, artistry). You're always drawn to something creative and consuming, and your Cancerian talents lend themselves to many different professions. But whatever the area, the secret to a *successful* career is that the work you do communicates an emotional message. You care a great deal about work, not only in the performance of it but in how much of your identity is wrapped up in it.

Work represents two things to you, self-esteem and security, and the security has to be both financial and emotional. No matter what kind of work you're in—whether high finance or performing on the stage—you are an imaginative, nurturing artist, and everything you do springs from your emotions. Therefore, to be emotionally centered in the work, to be connected by heartstrings, and to feel that it's an extension of family are the psychological linchpins of Cancer's relationship to work.

You are focused, intense, task oriented, and ambitious, which often surprises people because you can be so dreamy. Keep in mind you're a Water sign, filled with fantasy and feeling, but also a Cardinal sign—the only sign in the zodiac that is both. You're a creator *and* a go-getter. The jet-propulsion speed you exhibit when pursuing a goal can be astonishing.

Indeed, your ability to take action is a fundamental key to your success. You have the initiative to make necessary changes and to go forth with new plans. It's true that at times you have difficulty deciding *when* to make the first move. You weigh everything carefully: Is this the right moment? Is this what I really want? Certainly you're risk averse, but once you decide to take a gamble, you're off and running. And because you minimize risks by taking every precaution first, your gambles usually pay off.

You're a hard worker—when you've made a commitment to a responsibility, nothing and no one can persuade you to lessen your load. Also, getting the job done well is very important, and you have the persistence to see a difficult task through. You're a person of dedication who gives your utmost and is never satisfied with mediocre or halfway effort.

As for money, you understand the first rule of financial security: *in*come before *out*go. It surprises you to see how many things other people prefer to cold hard cash. In business, you're thrifty and farsighted, and you have a knack for making money grow. You are skilled at parlaying small sums into larger ones, and you also know how to make wise investments and where to get the best value.

You can be very work-driven, and need to make sure you do not lose yourself in work. The underlying psychological issue is that, for Cancer, work can become a substitute family that offers security and a sense of belonging. It has a great emotional hold on you and fosters your propensity (just as you do in relationships) for sacrificing yourself to it.

Specific careers for which you have an affinity flow out of your Cancerian interests. You enjoy activities that center on home and food—for example, being a chef or caterer, managing a restaurant, designing house interiors or gardens, or selling real estate. Cancer is a Water sign, and you have a fondness for the sea. You'd do well in the boating or nautical industry, or working on a cruise ship (e.g., being a tour director or onboard chef). You have a caring, healing touch, and occupations in medicine—such as being a physician, therapist, or nurse—utilize your natural-born talents. You excel in teaching (especially children). You have an eye for art and antiques, and are also drawn to music, acting, and writing.

For Cancer, a career is one of the most important ways life teaches you how powerful you are. It's in your career that you rely on your tenacity and excellent memory. You discover joy in your flair for performing. You develop faith in your talent for handling money. You learn you have creative originality and are blessed with a sixth sense of what the public will want. Small wonder that you tend to rise to positions of power in business and the arts.

CANCER AND HEALTH:
ADVICE FROM ASTROLOGY

For optimum health, Cancer needs a combination of recreation and relaxation. You tend to be a worrier, and life's daily problems bombard you from the outside while you struggle with inner nervousness and fear. You also tend to hold in your feelings. Secret grudges, anger, and painful memories take a huge toll on your health. Stresses from the outside and the inside worsen your anxiety and your depression. Tension also exacerbates a Cancerian predilection for stomach ailments. Exercise—especially the recreational kind—is both a mood lifter and energizer. Peaceful periods of relaxation are also an antidote. As a Cancer, you use food to soothe you psychologically, which only adds to problems with weight gain and digestion. You need to adhere to healthy eating habits and an exercise regime that's fun, invigorating, and gentle.

Advice and useful tips about health are among the most important kinds of information that astrology provides. Health and well-being are of paramount concern to human beings. Love, money, or career takes second place, for without good health we cannot enjoy anything in life.

Astrology and medicine have had a long marriage. Hippocrates (born around 460 B.C.), the Greek philosopher and physician who is considered the father of medicine, said, "A physician without a knowledge of astrology has no right to call himself a physician." Indeed, up until the eighteenth century, the study of astrology and its relationship to the body was very much a part of a doctor's training. When a patient became ill, a chart was immediately drawn up. This guided the doctor in both diagnosis and treatment, for the chart would tell when the crisis would come and what medicine would help. Of course, modern Western doctors no longer use astrology to treat illness. However, astrology can still be a useful tool in helping to understand and maintain our physical well-being.

THE PART OF THE BODY RULED BY CANCER

Each sign of the zodiac rules or governs a specific part of the body. These associations date back to the beginning of astrology. Curiously, the part of the body that a sign rules is in some ways the strongest and in other ways the weakest area for natives of that sign.

Your sign of Cancer rules the breasts and the stomach. This part of the anatomy has always symbolized nourishment and motherhood, and you are characterized as protective and clinging. Cancer women often have beautiful bosoms, with soft, creamy skin and a curving décolletage. Cancer men have well-shaped chests and flat stomachs. Whichever gender you are, all this changes as you grow older, for you're susceptible to gaining weight in later years. You find it very difficult to lose excess weight.

Tension, anxiety, and emotional stress are the leading cause of illness among natives of your sign. You have a delicate stomach and tend to have digestive problems. You're prone to ulcers, gallbladder upsets, gas pains, nausea, and gastritis. Your health is not especially robust, particularly in childhood, and you're inclined to suffer from upper respiratory infections such as bronchitis. Born under a Water sign, your lungs and sinuses tend to hold in fluid. Also as a Water sign, your proclivity is to overindulge in alcohol, which you do not tolerate well. Drinking alcohol aggravates your stomach problems, increases weight, and causes fluid retention in body tissues.

The Moon, ruler of Cancer, has dominion over the breasts and the alimentary canal, heightening your susceptibility in these areas.

DIET AND HEALTH TIPS FOR CANCER

Food means security to you, and when you're feeling low you tend to go on eating binges. You turn to pies, cakes, ice cream, candy, and potato chips to make yourself feel better. This is a self-accelerating spiral, for excess sweets and salty carbohydrates make your stomach worse. You need to watch your diet very carefully in order to keep your digestive system healthy and your weight under control.

The cell salt* for Cancer is calcium fluoride, which unites with albumen and oil in the body's system to keep elastic and connective tissues healthy. It is also an important ingredient in tooth enamel, fingernails, bones, and the lens of the eye. Deficiency of

*Cell salts (also known as tissue salts) are mineral compounds found in human tissue cells. These minerals are the only substances our cells cannot produce by themselves. The life of cells is relatively short, and the creation of new cells depends on the presence of these minerals.

this mineral can cause varicose veins, receding gums, curvature of the spine, eye problems, and cataracts. Food sources for calcium fluoride are egg yolks, whole-grain rye, yogurt, beets, watercress, fish, and oysters.

You're prone to skin disorders when there is a lack of calcium in your diet. You should consume milk, cheese, kale, lettuce, and tomatoes, which are high in calcium. Okra, which also contains calcium, is an aid in reducing stomach inflammations. Fresh vegetables, fresh fruit, and lean protein are a daily must. Starches, sugar, and salt produce bloat. You should stay away from spicy, highly seasoned food and should forgo hot-pepper sauce and horseradish.

Always have your meals in pleasant surroundings—no bickering or heated discussions at the dinner table. Taking a walk after a meal aids digestion and serenity of mind. Walking in warm rain (under an umbrella) or by the seashore is excellent, for the moist air soothes the lungs.

If you get sick, you recuperate faster in your own bed at home.

THE DECANATES AND CUSPS OF CANCER

Decanate and *cusp* are astrological terms that subdivide your Sun sign. These subdivisions further define and emphasize certain qualities and character traits of your Sun sign Cancer.

WHAT IS A DECANATE?

Each astrological sign is divided into three parts, and each part is called a *decanate* or a *decan* (the terms are used interchangeably).

The word comes from the Greek word *dekanoi*, meaning "ten days apart." The Greeks took their word from the Egyptians, who divided their year into 360 days.* The Egyptian year had twelve months of thirty days each, and each month was further divided into three sections of ten days each. It was these ten-day sections that the Greeks called *dekanoi*.

*The Egyptians soon found out that a 360-day year was inaccurate, and so added on five extra days. These were feast days and holidays, and not counted as real days.

Astrology still divides the zodiac into decanates. There are twelve signs in the zodiac, and each sign is divided into three decanates. You might picture each decanate as a room. You were born in the sign of Cancer, which consists of three rooms (decanates). In which room of Cancer were you born?

The zodiac is a 360-degree circle. Each decanate is ten degrees of that circle, or about ten days long, since the Sun moves through the zodiac at approximately the rate of one degree per day. (This is not exact, because not all of our months contain thirty days.)

The decanate of a sign does not change the basic characteristics of that sign, but it does refine and individualize the sign's general characteristics. If you were born, say, in the second decanate of Cancer, it does not change the fact that you are Cancer. It does indicate that you have somewhat special characteristics, different from those of Cancer people born in the first decanate or the third decanate.

Finally, each decanate has a specific planetary ruler, sometimes called a subruler because it does not usurp the overall rulership of your sign. The subruler can only enhance and add to the distinct characteristics of your decanate. For example, your entire sign of Cancer is ruled by the Moon, but the second decanate of Cancer is subruled by Pluto. The influence of Pluto, the subruler, combines with the overall authority of the Moon to make the second decanate of Cancer unlike any other in the zodiac.

FIRST DECANATE OF CANCER

June 21 through June 30
Keyword: Receptiveness

Constellation: Canis Minor, the Small Dog, who symbolizes reason.
Planetary subruler: The Moon

The Moon is both your ruler and subruler, and so you tend to be very receptive and sensitive to other people. You see deeply into human nature, and your insights and guidance are often sought after. You would make an excellent teacher or instructor. Rationality is important to you. Even though you are an emotional person, you are able to sift through facts and arrive at a fair decision. You have an excellent memory for feelings and impressions (both yours and those of others), but ordinary day-to-day details escape you. In relationships, you look for harmony and security. You dislike quarrels and dissension, and any kind of emotional disturbance leaves you depressed. At times you are too moody and pessimistic.

SECOND DECANATE OF CANCER

July 1 through July 11
Keyword: Intensity
Constellation: Canis Major, the Great Dog, companion to the mighty hunter Orion. He symbolizes triumph.
Planetary subruler: Pluto

Pluto is the planet of depth and intensity, and combines with your Cancer Moon to give you a forceful yet thoughtful personality. Of the three Cancer decanates, yours is the most mystical and the most interested in things unseen. People are drawn to your sensitivity and often tell you their secrets. Your intellectual talents are formidable, even though your strong feelings predominate when making decisions. Both curious and intuitive, you are able to gather facts and information from all sources and use them for your benefit. In work, you are disciplined and practical; in relationships, you are the opposite—sentimental, emotional, and often possessive. You have a tendency to become too fixed and rigid once you've set your mind.

THIRD DECANATE OF CANCER

July 12 through July 22
Keyword: Empathy
Constellation: Argo Navis, the magical ship of adventure that symbolizes strength of mind. Placed in the heavens by Poseidon to be a guide to travelers on the southern seas.
Planetary subruler: Neptune

The spiritual planet Neptune is your subruler, which joins forces with Cancer's Moon to accentuate an impressionable and romantic nature. You may be very artistic, and you try to create beauty and harmony around you. Your adaptability to different kinds of people is one of your secrets of success. Many of you are destined for some kind of public life. You have the ability to touch people's feelings and to form close ties. These bonds may take time to develop, but they tend to last forever. In love, you have deep emotions. You are loyal and protective toward your family and mate, and you believe only the best about them. Cautious and conservative are the words that best describe your approach to problems. Even in the midst of crisis, you look for balance. Often you are prone toward discontent and dissatisfaction.

WHAT IS A CUSP?

A cusp is the point at which a new astrological sign begins.* Thus, the cusp of Cancer means the point at which Cancer begins. (The word comes from the Latin word *cuspis*, meaning "point.")

When someone speaks of being "born on the cusp," that person is referring to a birth time at or near the beginning or the end of an astrological sign. For example, if you were born on July 22, you were born on the cusp of Leo, the sign that begins on July 23. Indeed, depending on what year you were born, your birth time might even be in the first degree of Leo. People born on the very day a sign begins or ends are often confused about what sign they really are—a confusion made more complicated by the fact that the Sun does not move into or out of a sign at *exactly* the same moment (or even day) each year. There are slight time differences from year to year. Therefore, if you are a Cancer born on June 21 or July 22, you'll find great clarity consulting a computer chart that tells you exactly where the Sun was at the very moment you were born.

As for what span of time constitutes being born on the cusp, the astrological community holds various opinions. Some astrologers claim cusp means being born only within the first two days or last two days of a sign (though many say this is too narrow a time frame). Others say it can be as much as within the first ten days or last ten days of a sign (which many say is too wide an interpretation). The consensus is that you were born on the cusp if your birthday is within the first *five* days or last *five* days of a sign.

*In a birth chart, a cusp is also the point at which an astrological House begins.

The question hanging over cusp-born people is, "What sign am I really?" They feel they straddle the border of two different countries. To some extent, this is true. If you were born on the cusp, you're under the influence of both signs. However, much like being a traveler leaving one country and crossing into another, you must actually *be* in one country—you can't be in two countries at the same time. One sign is always a stronger influence, and that sign is almost invariably the sign that the Sun was actually in (in other words, your Sun sign). The reason I say "almost" is that in rare cases a chart may be so heavily weighted with planets in a certain sign that the person more keenly feels the influence of that specific sign.

For example, I have a client who was born in the evening on July 22. On that evening, the Sun was leaving Cancer and entering Leo. At the moment of her birth, the Sun was still in Cancer, so technically speaking she is a Cancer. However, the Sun was only a couple hours away from being in Leo, and this person has the Moon, Mercury, and Venus all in Leo. She has always felt like a Leo and has always behaved as a Leo.

This, obviously, is an unusual case. Generally, the Sun is the most powerful planetary influence in a chart. Even if you were born with the Sun on the very tip of the first or last degree of Cancer, Cancer is your Sun sign—and this is the sign you will most feel like.

Still, the influence of the approaching sign or of the sign just ending is present, and you will probably sense that mixture in yourself.

BORN JUNE 21 THROUGH JUNE 25

You are Cancer with Gemini tendencies. You have a sympathetic and generous nature, and an incisive, intellectual mind. You may be famous for your brain, but those close to you know you are a softie inside. Sometimes your heart and mind are at odds with each other; emotions affect you more than you like to admit. You have a special touch for getting along with people from all walks of life. You need stimulation and change, and will become discontent if stuck in one place for too long.

BORN JULY 18 THROUGH JULY 22

You are Cancer with Leo tendencies. You are idealistic and sensitive, and also clever and forceful, and you probably have a temper that quickly comes and goes. In work, you like doing things your own way. You possess a pleasing social grace that mixes easily with people, but you take a long time to form truly close relationships. Love is not impulsive. You may be instantly attracted to someone, but you are careful because you fear rejection and won't let yourself become too vulnerable.

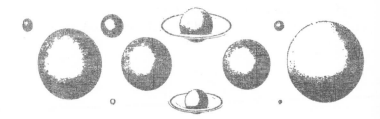

YOUR SPECIAL DAY OF BIRTH

JUNE 21

You are sharp-witted and a wonderful entertainer and, unlike many Cancerians, able to forgive and forget. Basically, you're obsessed with life, eager to experience everything and love passionately.

JUNE 22

You need freedom and variety along with stability. You have unusual creative talents—your intuitive understanding of people gives you an edge in your work. In love, you're a deep romantic under a cynical shell.

JUNE 23

You have a magnetic personality full of fantasy and seduction. In time, you learn to care more about your commitments than people's opinions of you. Finding the soulmate you seek is elusive, but you absolutely will.

JUNE 24

You're a mystic and a poet yet such a realist that most people don't see your magical side. You have flair with the public and your work will make money. In love, you'll reach a crossroads and then make the right decision.

JUNE 25

People gravitate to your sparkling originality—you're famous for your wit—but your closest inner circle is carefully chosen. You're deeply feeling; when you truly love, you love forever. You're a handful when you're crabby.

JUNE 26

You must never doubt you're blessed with inner strength. You're adept intellectually and physically, and therefore are a thinker *and* a doer. You have a creative approach to life, and your love passions are tumultuous.

JUNE 27

You were born to shine in an unusual project, venture, or adventure. Your outlook and opinions have a tremendous effect on others. You have an intuitive heart, and can read the feelings of someone you love.

JUNE 28

You may think you lack confidence but the world sees you as bold and assertive. Your humor is outrageous, your thinking incisive, and your heart giving. In love, you need reassurance and deep sexual connection.

JUNE 29

You give the impression of *flying*—you're imaginative, full of ideas, on the go. Yet, oddly, you procrastinate about important things. In love, you're impetuous, not always careful about choosing someone loyal.

JUNE 30

You stand out because of your one-of-a-kind talent. In work, you're an incisive thinker; in emotional life you're nurturing. Your passions can become obsessive. At some point you will choose between staying and leaving.

JULY 1

You were born with charismatic radiance, yet you're private and extraordinarily sensitive. You must guard against taking on others' feelings as yours. In love, you're protective, loyal, and often too long-suffering.

JULY 2

You're exciting, enlivening, a catalyst for change. You're a fixer in others' lives. In work, you're drawn to the untried path. In romance, you offer emotional richness—be sure to choose someone worthy of your love splendor.

JULY 3

You're self-protective but appear to be open and genial. Creatively, you have a critical eye and can write and speak effectively. In love, you communicate through affection, sex, and touch as well as words.

JULY 4

You have freshness, vivacity, and an openness to people. But you hide turbulent emotions and are more complicated than you seem. You have theatrical creativity. Your affections are extravagant, and love can be chaotic.

JULY 5

You love to ask questions and people adore you. Use your ability to tune into public taste, and you can make good money. In love, you're irrepressibly romantic, utterly passionate, and a touch unstable.

JULY 6

Old textbooks name this day "Magnetic Desire." You have an artist's soul and achieve your life's purpose when you immerse yourself in a project you love. Romantically, you give with passion. Be careful about boundaries.

JULY 7

In work, you're a high-principled go-getter, and in friendship a trusted confidante. You're tenacious, and love brings out your possessive streak. Learn to let go, and you'll find the happiness you're destined for.

JULY 8

You're interested in ideas and ideals, and in work highly responsible. Yet you're also never quite content no matter where you are or whom you're with. Love can get complicated, for you're courageous but also easily entangled.

JULY 9

You're curious and inventive, and have an original way of expressing yourself. Your work will be recognized by a large number of people. You're a profound romantic with a tendency to withdraw into the relationship.

JULY 10

You have mischievous talent to amuse—yet you're also somewhat detached and introverted. In love, you're self-protective but very passionate when you let down your guard. You're destined to make a life-decision that surprises everyone.

JULY 11

You're alluring, gregarious, have social flair—and also high ethics. In your career, the spotlight finds you even when you try to hide. In love, you're totally honest and therefore need someone who always tells the truth.

JULY 12

You're persuasive, though to you you're only speaking your mind. In business, you're persistent and shrewd—and tend to control others (perhaps too much). You come alive when in love; you're a great support to your lover.

JULY 13

You're smart about how the world works and able to spot opportunity. Oddly you're also an innocent who can be taken advantage of in love. Your life-lesson is to learn whom to trust (and whom not to). You have powerful emotions.

JULY 14

Immensely creative, you can write, act, perform, or start a new business. You have huge seductive powers both in work and in love. Once you get a handle on your mood-swings, you'll find deep happiness with a soulmate.

JULY 15

You're influential and dynamic, though you see yourself as shy. A great gift is your receptive mind—you allow inspiration in. Emotionally, you're intense, unforgiving, and very sexual when you're in love.

JULY 16

You have a soft heart for others, but for yourself are an exacting taskmaster. You do best working on your own and are promised financial gain. Love brings out your raw emotions; you must beware of unscrupulous lovers.

JULY 17

No matter what company you're in, you're able to relate. You have a common touch but a connoisseur's elegance—a wonderful mix of the everyman and the noble. In work, you exhibit fertile imagination, and in love you need intense passion.

JULY 18

You're caring and sympathetic, and are able to get to the emotional truth of another person. This makes you a sleuth in your work and a comrade in friendship. In love, though, you lose your heart quickly and must guard against being taken advantage of.

JULY 19

You're a quick study, and when you take a wild chance you often open a successful path. You're mystical and spiritual, yet people describe you as a bon vivant. It takes a special lover to help you release your pent-up passion.

JULY 20

You have extraordinary talent and fierce determination. Around you is a tinge of sadness; be careful not to compromise in order to be taken care of. In love, you're pulled between security and the wild unknown.

JULY 21

You're elegant, communicative, and funny all at the same time. You want a placid life but have a way of attracting complications. Emotionally you're a risk taker, and your love life is a series of fascinating dramas.

You strive for order and control and yet your life is filled with ups and downs and adventures others don't have. You're a curious mix of reliability and rebellion. You need secure love but tend to lose yourself to passion.

YOU AND CHINESE ASTROLOGY

With Marco Polo's adventurous travels in A.D. 1275, Europeans learned for the first time of the great beauty, wealth, history, and romance of China. Untouched as they were by outside influences, the Chinese developed their astrology along different lines from other ancient cultures, such as the Egyptians, Babylonians, and Greeks in whose traditions Western astrology has its roots. Therefore the Chinese zodiac differs from the zodiac of the West. To begin with, it's based on a lunar cycle rather than Western astrology's solar cycle. The Chinese zodiac is divided into twelve years, and each year is represented by a different animal—the rat, ox, tiger, rabbit, dragon, snake, horse, goat, monkey, rooster, dog, or pig. The legend of the twelve animals is that when Buddha lay on his deathbed, he asked the animals of the forest to come and bid him farewell. These twelve were the first to arrive. The cat, as the story goes, is not among the animals because it was napping and couldn't be bothered to make the journey. (In some Asian countries, however, such as Vietnam, the cat replaces the rabbit.)

Like Western astrology, in which the zodiac signs have different characteristics, each of the twelve Chinese animal years assigns character traits specific to a person born in that year. For example, the Year of the Rat confers honesty and an analytical mind, whereas the Year of the Monkey grants charm and a quick ability to spot opportunity.

Here are descriptions for Cancer for each Chinese animal year:

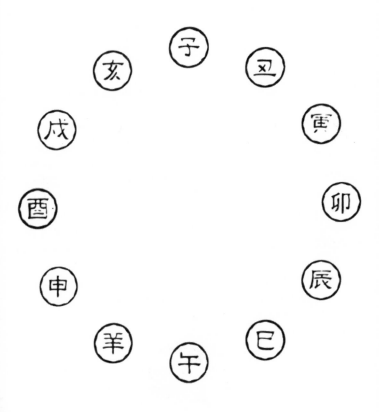

Years of the Rat

1900	1960	2020	2080
1912	1972	2032	2092
1924	1984	2044	
1936	1996	2056	
1948	2008	2068	

In the West, rats are not highly regarded, but in Asia the Rat is courageous and extremely inventive, and possesses devastating charm. These Rat qualities blend beautifully with your Cancerian creativity and ability to spot opportunity. The Rat is associated with new beginnings, which works well with Cancer being a Cardinal sign (an initiator). As a Cancer Rat you have an enterprising spirit and are extra clever about ideas that make money. You have a broad range of interests and a magical way with people, qualities that make you a good executive. More than other Cancerians, you're comfortable with delegating, though it's certainly true you can be meddling, irritable, and anxious. In love, you're at your best, capable of deep commitment and being a giving, passionate lover. Compatible partners are born in the Years of the Monkey, Pig, Rat, and Snake.

IF YOU ARE CANCER BORN IN THE YEAR OF THE OX

Years of the Ox

1901	1961	2021	2081
1913	1973	2033	2093
1925	1985	2045	
1937	1997	2057	
1949	2009	2069	

The Chinese associate lovely qualities with the Ox—elegance, eloquence, diligence, dignity. Being born in the Year of the Ox is said to confer nobility and a sense of purpose. Definitely, Ox intelligence and levelheadedness integrate wonderfully with your Cancerian striving to give your best and your special talent for creating stability. As a Cancer Ox you're also known for being innovative and imaginative—which certainly are Cancerian traits, but which are made more *practical* by being an Ox. Try to avoid the negatives of avariciousness or falling into gloomy thinking. Your Cancer moodiness is underscored. Romantically, however, being a Cancer Ox allows you to express profound sensuality. Be careful not to give yourself away too easily, for you invest yourself completely. Compatible partners are born in the Years of the Rabbit, Rooster, Monkey, Pig, and Snake.

IF YOU ARE CANCER BORN IN THE YEAR OF THE TIGER

Years of the Tiger

1902	1962	2022	2082
1914	1974	2034	2094
1926	1986	2046	
1938	1998	2058	
1950	2010	2070	

The Tiger is a superstar of the Chinese zodiac—magnetic, fueled by take-charge energy, destined to live life with style. The charismatic creativity of the Tiger blends seamlessly with your Cancerian artist's eye and ability to seize the moment. Additionally, your tenacity is emphasized, as well as your emotional approach (to projects, people, partnerships). To Buddhists the Tiger symbolizes the power of faith, and this intensity underlines your Cancer Tiger character. Having to answer to anyone galls you, and you're best off being your own boss. As a Cancer you dislike risk, yet the Tiger in you will take a chance with a big idea. In love, you're passionate and possessive, though you have a roving eye as well as issues with trust. Compatible partners are born in the Years of the Rabbit, Dog, Dragon, Monkey, Pig, and Tiger.

IF YOU ARE CANCER BORN IN THE YEAR OF THE RABBIT

Years of the Rabbit

1903	1963	2023	2083
1915	1975	2035	2095
1927	1987	2047	
1939	1999	2059	
1951	2011	2071	

Far from being a timid creature, the Asian Rabbit is theatrical, talkative, sophisticated, and brilliant at handling an audience. Your Cancerian ability to read people is heightened, and you're skilled at business. In Chinese astrology, the Rabbit is linked to the Moon—as Cancer is in Western astrology—doubly emphasizing the Moon quality of a fertile imagination. You're admired, trusted, and a gifted diplomat who keeps peace between warring factions. Curiously, you yourself are thin-skinned and easily hurt, and must guard against becoming aloof when you feel threatened. In your romantic life, you're affectionate and flirtatious, and you like sexual fantasy. You would love to be swept away by grand passion. Compatible partners are born in the Years of the Goat, Dog, Dragon, Snake, Horse, and Monkey.

IF YOU ARE CANCER BORN IN THE YEAR OF THE DRAGON

Years of the Dragon

1904	1964	2024	2084
1916	1976	2036	2096
1928	1988	2048	
1940	2000	2060	
1952	2012	2072	

In China, the Dragon is a divine beast filled with mythic power. It symbolizes the quest to live a magnanimous life—and being born in a Dragon year bestows high ideals and optimism that's hard to quench. As a Cancerian, you're already imaginative and expressive—and this added to Dragon ambition makes you both creative *and* commanding. People emulate your style; you aren't aware how much of a role model you are. You're a creature of intense feelings. Fight those bouts of dissatisfaction when you don't get all your wants met. Also, because you lead from the heart instead of the head, be careful about whom you align with in business and in love. You're a passionate and sexually dramatic lover who praises a mate to the skies, and you are surprisingly vulnerable. Compatible partners are born in the Years of the Rabbit, Goat, Monkey, Snake, and Tiger.

Years of the Snake

1905	1965	2025	2085
1917	1977	2037	2097
1929	1989	2049	
1941	2001	2061	
1953	2013	2073	

In Asian mythology, the Snake is the adored companion of the Goddess of Love, Beauty, and the Sea. The Snake is wise, beautiful, and full of grace and extraordinary talent. As it is, you are the Water sign of Cancer who excels in expressing what's in your imagination, and as a Cancer Snake you are doubly fluent. You're artistic, have star quality, have great initiative, and are a master manipulator of public opinion. You exhibit assurance and strong opinions; you're a performer. Underneath it all is a complicated and complex emotional life. You're deeply feeling and search for completion (in work and love) to fill a sense of loneliness. You're a sensualist, and love can become obsessive, though you're capable of lasting devotion. Compatible partners are born in the Years of the Rabbit, Rooster, Dragon, Horse, Ox, and Rat.

IF YOU ARE CANCER BORN IN THE YEAR OF THE HORSE

Years of the Horse

1906	1966	2026	2086
1918	1978	2038	2098
1930	1990	2050	
1942	2002	2062	
1954	2014	2074	

The Horse symbolizes the power possessed by gods and heroes. In China, pregnancies are planned around a Horse year because a child is promised success. Being born in the Year of the Horse is said to bestow high intelligence, popularity, persuasiveness, and a love of adventure. Horse charisma added to your Cancerian entrepreneurial energy makes you a spark plug in creative work. You're original in your thinking and unconventional in your projects. You can be a hot-blooded rebel when those of lesser talents try to confine you in their boxes. Socially, you have a large coterie of friends from different walks of life. In love, you yearn to *belong*; yet, because you're independent, finding the one who understands your deep passions and questing heart is an elusive goal. Compatible partners are born in the Years of the Rabbit, Rooster, Goat, Horse, and Snake.

IF YOU ARE CANCER BORN IN THE YEAR OF THE GOAT

Years of the Goat

1907	1967	2027	2087
1919	1979	2039	2099
1931	1991	2051	
1943	2003	2063	
1955	2015	2075	

In the Chinese zodiac, the Goat is the sage, famed for its wisdom and good judgment. Born in a Goat Year, you have a razor-sharp mind and a sweet, generous heart. Being Cancer, you're deeply intuitive to begin with, and extra Goat qualities, such as the ability to decipher patterns in people and relationships, make you someone others gravitate to for advice. In addition, you're a doer who can bring ideas to life. You work hard, have elegant taste, and are persevering—Cancer traits intensified. But as a Cancer Goat, you also tend to be dissatisfied. You fantasize about romantic adventure and erotic abandon, though oddly you're shy. You compensate for this by being very friendly and don't release your sexuality unless you're feeling safe. Compatible partners are born in the Years of the Rabbit, Dragon, Horse, Monkey, and Pig.

IF YOU ARE CANCER BORN IN THE YEAR OF THE MONKEY

申

Years of the Monkey

1908	1968	2028	2088
1920	1980	2040	2100
1932	1992	2052	
1944	2004	2064	
1956	2016	2076	

In Chinese mythology, the Monkey accompanies the God of Travel to help drive away boredom. The Monkey is curious, vivacious, witty, and whimsical, and you, born in the Year of the Monkey, blend these felicitous qualities with your Cancer intelligence and imagination. The Cancer Monkey is known as the "changeable genius"—you're brilliant and quick-thinking, and you easily adapt to new situations. You're an actor at heart. You can cover up your real feelings and subtly maneuver people. You're great fun to be with, though beneath the charm is a will of steel. Usually you employ this to set changes into motion and achieve your goals. In love, you can be a puzzle. You may plunge into an all-consuming passion and then suddenly distance yourself. Compatible partners are born in the Years of the Rabbit, Dragon, Ox, Pig, Rat, and Tiger.

IF YOU ARE CANCER BORN IN THE YEAR OF THE ROOSTER

Years of the Rooster

1909	1957	2005	2053
1921	1969	2017	2065
1933	1981	2029	2077
1945	1993	2041	2089

In Asia, the Rooster (who in mythology rescued the Sun goddess) has always symbolized courage and audacity. Roosters are said to be outspoken, multitalented, resilient, full of pizzazz, and undaunted in the face of difficulty. Chinese teachings say that Roosters know how to "resist despair." This important trait, when added to your Cancerian stick-to-it-iveness, makes you a formidable achiever. You're also less moody than other Cancers, though certainly you can be feisty and obstinate. Actually, as a Cancer Rooster you have the reputation of a delightful eccentric, one who develops fascinating interests and goes your own way. In love, you're very honest, very black-and-white. You don't play emotional games. You're loyal, passionate, and romantic. Compatible partners are born in the Years of the Horse, Ox, and Snake.

IF YOU ARE CANCER BORN IN THE YEAR OF THE DOG

Years of the Dog

1910	1958	2006	2054
1922	1970	2018	2066
1934	1982	2030	2078
1946	1994	2042	2090

As with the real-life animal, the Asian Dog is treasured for its fidelity and devotion. Being born in the Year of the Dog grants you heroism, honesty, a caring heart, and a sweet nature—essentially, you're *lovable*. The Dog sense of duty melds with your Cancerian generosity to make you extra attentive to others' needs. Be careful, however, to pay equal attention to your own needs—and guard against pessimism. As a Cancer Dog, you're a quick study and a hard worker, and your Cancerian creativity is magnified. Because you inspire confidence, you're also good at organizing groups and resolving problems. Emotionally, you tend to open up only to those you trust, although this has not saved you from heartbreak. Still, long term you're promised deep happiness in love. Compatible partners are born in the Years of the Rabbit, Dog, Pig, and Tiger.

IF YOU ARE CANCER BORN IN THE YEAR OF THE PIG

Years of the Pig

1911	1959	2007	2055
1923	1971	2019	2067
1935	1983	2031	2079
1947	1995	2043	2091

In the West, the pig is held in low esteem, but in Asia the Pig is gallant, chivalrous, cultured, and knowledgeable. If you were born in the Year of the Pig, you're described as intellectual, strong, a person of fortitude willing to give your best to whatever you undertake. The honesty and high principles of the Pig magnify your Cancerian passion to lead a life that counts for something. You have visionary ideas that you pursue determinedly, and more than a little luck financially. Some might say you're a tad materialistic, and, though you're peaceable at heart, when crossed you can be a boar. As a friend, you're a Rock of Gibraltar. Romantically, you're a sensuous voluptuary who longs for unconditional love. You need to learn to choose lovers who won't take advantage of you. Compatible partners are born in the Years of the Rabbit, Dog, Pig, and Tiger.

YOU AND NUMEROLOGY

Numerology is the language of numbers. It is the belief that there is a correlation between numbers and living things, ideas, and concepts. Certainly, numbers surround and infuse our lives (e.g., twenty-four hours in a day, twelve months of the year, etc.). And from ancient times mystics have taught that numbers carry a *vibration*, a deeper meaning that defines how each of us fits into the universe. According to numerology, you are born with a personal number that contains information about who you are and what you need to be happy. This number expresses what numerology calls your life path.

All numbers reduce to one of nine digits, numbers 1 through 9. Your personal number is based on your date of birth. To calculate your number, write your birth date in numerals. As an example, the birth date of June 29, 1983, is written 6-29-1983. Now begin the addition: 6 + 29 + 1 + 9 + 8 + 3 = 56; 56 reduces to 5 + 6 = 11; 11 reduces to 1 + 1 = 2. The personal number for someone born June 29, 1983, is *Two*.

IF YOU ARE A CANCER ONE

Keywords: Confidence and Creativity

One is the number of new beginnings, which magnifies your Cancerian initiative powers. You rush into whatever engages your emotions and are especially keen to start on a creative project. You're attracted to unusual pursuits because you like to be one-of-a-kind—and don't like to be under the thumb of other people's whims. However, you have a lovely gift for fostering warm relationships. In all you do, you're known for being *real*, expressing who you are. In love, you're courageous and will choose a path others may advise against because you feel the rightness in your heart. You're a passionate romantic.

IF YOU ARE A CANCER TWO

Keywords: Cooperation and Balance

Two is the number of cooperation and creating a secure entity. You are *magnetic*—you attract what you need and gather in. Your magic is not only your people skills, but your ability to breathe life into empty forms (e.g., a concept, an ambitious business idea, a new relationship) and produce something of worth. With determination and persistence, you attain material things, loyal friendships, and heartfelt love connections. You are passionately creative and enjoy music, the arts, and gardening. In love, your deepest desire is for a committed partnership with someone you can trust and share confidences with.

IF YOU ARE A CANCER THREE

Keywords: Expression and Sensitivity

Three symbolizes self-expression. You have a joyful personality, a gift for words, and a talent for visualization. Three is the number of the "connector." You link people together so that they benefit from each other. You motivate others and make them think. Imaginative creativity is your specialty and you have a deep need to be involved—you don't like being a solitary looker-on. Your quest is to excel at doing things a little differently; you bring tradition to new ways of thinking. In love, you need someone who excites you intellectually and also fills your passionate sensuality. You need a *soulmate*.

IF YOU ARE A CANCER FOUR

Keywords: Stability and Process

Four is the number of dedication and loyalty. It represents *foundation*, exactly as the four-sided square does that symbolizes Four. This strengthens your Cancer ability to build security. First you plan, then day-by-day you add the next step, the next layer, keeping on schedule. You're persistent—and therefore able to control your environment, accomplish great works, and achieve high honor. One of your nicest qualities is your caring commitment to others. Your style of loving is to invest yourself wholly. Romantically, you adore closeness and being enclosed in a downy quilt of security.

IF YOU ARE A CANCER FIVE

Keywords: Freedom and Discipline

Five is the number of change and freedom, which is most apparent in your mental brilliance. With your chameleon intellect (it can go in any direction) and ability to deal with people, you're a marvelous *persuader*. You influence others and have great skill with the public. In relationships, you give generously—but unlike many Cancerians, you don't get stuck in the role of the sacrificer. Success comes to you because you're able to let go of what doesn't work, especially in your career. Romantically, you need a lover with whom you can communicate—someone who energizes your creativity and sparks your vibrant sensuality.

IF YOU ARE A CANCER SIX

Keywords: Vision and Acceptance

Six is the number of teaching, healing, and utilizing your talents. You're geared toward changing the world or at least fixing other people's lives. Being an advice-giver and even a therapist to your friends comes naturally. Love really does rule your universe, but your life is not just sweetness and light. You can be exacting and demanding—especially with yourself. You're your own harshest critic, for you hold yourself up to a standard of excellence. In love, you're fervent about being a helpmate and confidante, as well as a lover. You're also a secret sensualist who gives your all to someone you trust.

IF YOU ARE A CANCER SEVEN

Keywords: Trust and Openness

Seven is the number of the mystic and the intensely focused specialist. You have an instinct for problem-solving, and in a flash understand how things work (in business, between people, etc.). You're both an intellectual and a connoisseur of everything creative. Your work, however, is only part of a deeper search for trust in yourself. You ponder life and have a philosophical bent. At your core you're extremely loyal and intensely loving, though very selective about relationships. In love, your deepest need is for a partner who understands your complex heart and can help you in your journey to becoming the real you.

IF YOU ARE A CANCER EIGHT

Keywords: Abundance and Power

Eight is the number of mastery and authority. You are intelligent and alert, born to take control in your own hands and guide traffic into the direction you want. Not as diffident as many Cancerians, you have special leadership ability. You work well in groups because you see what's needed and others sense you're the one who knows best. As a Cancer Eight, you're totally true to your word. Giving your promise in love is a very serious act. You are a protective and deeply caring lover, and need to know your lover is your unwavering ally. Your inner drive is to create a stable base with someone you adore and respect.

Keywords: Integrity and Wisdom

Nine is the path of the "old soul," the number of completion and full bloom. Because it's the last number, it sums up the highs and lows of human experience, and you live a life of dramatic events. You're very intellectual, deeply feeling, extremely protective, interested in acquiring all kinds of knowledge. You channel your energy into what is captivating, worthwhile, and lasting. People see you as heroic and altruistic. In love, you're truthful and sincere—and also a romantic, highly sensual creature. As a Cancer Nine you generously give of yourself, often to the point of being sacrificing.

LAST WORD: YOUR CANCER UNFINISHED BUSINESS

Psychologists often use the phrase *unfinished business* to describe unresolved issues—for example, patterns from childhood that cause unhappiness, anger that keeps one stuck, or scenarios of family dysfunction that repeat through second and third generations (such as alcoholism or abusive behavior).

Astrology teaches that the past is indeed very much with us in the present. And that using astrological insights can help us move out of emotional darkness into greater clarity. Even within this book (which is not a tome of hundreds of pages) you have read of many of the superlatives and challenges of being Cancer. You have breathtaking gifts, and at the same time certain tendencies that can undermine utilizing these abilities.

In nature, a fascinating fact is that in jungles and forests a poisonous plant will grow in a certain spot, and always just a few feet away is a plant that is the antidote to that specific poison. Likewise, in astrology, the antidote is right there, ready to be used when the negatives threaten to overwhelm your life.

Cancer's unfinished business has to do with *enclosure*. Like the other two Water signs, Scorpio and Pisces, you want to merge. But unlike Scorpio, who wants to meld sexually/spiritually, or Pisces, who wants to create a relationship apart from rough-and-tumble reality, you want to preserve and keep the safe cocoon of your bonding. Psychologically, you operate on the theory that letting go means loss—that you will be left alone, that you will lose that person's love—and that if you try hard enough, the other will want to be as close as you do. None of this may be in your conscious mind, but it certainly lies beneath the surface.

You're highly threatened if someone you care for wants to move out of your enclosed space. Your way of showing love is to be a protective mother hen. Yet it is *you* that you are actually protecting. You guard yourself against your fears by gathering people, family, friendships, lovers, and, of course, money and possessions to yourself.

Further, Cancer is an emotional sign (some would say overemotional). Whatever you enter into—career projects, relationships, plans—you do so leading with your emotions. You rush forward with heady enthusiasm, or you're dejected over a presumed injury, or you are plowing through a miasma of worries. At times you're overwrought, exhausted by struggling with inner chaos.

Yet the antidotes are there, to be found in their entirety in being Cancer—in your extraordinary creativity and your power to love. Among your key strengths are the force of your imagination and the intensity of your caring.

When you're able to get beyond *self* ("I need, I want, I will keep") and extend your caring to a wider world—whether this is in your work or artistry or relationships, or in doing something to change society—you are a power source unlike anyone else.

When you're able to value yourself as much as you value the "security" of a love relationship, you will create the right partnership. When you pay attention to early danger signals from someone less than honorable instead of wanting so much to be taken care of that you ignore them, you will be safe.

You can counter your fear—the basic root of what holds you back. Ask yourself, "What is the worst that can happen?" "What if I lose this?" "What if I don't get this?" Tap into your Cancer courage to look fear in the face. By considering where you would be if the thing you crave fell away, you will find your own essential strength. You will see what you truly *have*. You are powerful and wise, blessed with the ability to peer through the shadowy ordinariness of others and discover possibility.

Use your Cancer ability to *see* and then to *act*—this is your unfinished business.

FAMOUS PEOPLE WITH THE SUN IN CANCER

Alexander the Great
Louis Armstrong
Polly Bergen
Ingmar Bergman
Bill Blass
David Brinkley
Mel Brooks
Yul Brynner
George W. Bush
James Cagney
Pierre Cardin
Barbara Cartland
Marc Chagall
Gower Champion
John Chancellor
Van Cliburn
Jean Cocteau
Bill Cosby
Tom Cruise
Olivia de Havilland
Oscar de la Renta
Diana, Princess of Wales
Phyllis Diller
Marty Feldman
M. F. K. Fisher
Harrison Ford
Bob Fosse
Stephen Foster
Erle Stanley Gardner
John Glenn
Merv Griffin
Susan Hayward

Nathaniel Hawthorne
Ernest Hemingway
Al Hirschfeld
Judy Holliday
Lena Horne
Anjelica Huston
Randy Jackson
Derek Jeter
Frida Kahlo
Franz Kafka
Helen Keller
Rose Kennedy
Ann Landers
Janet Leigh
Lindsay Lohan
Gina Lollobrigida
Sidney Lumet
Tobey Maguire
Nelson Mandela
Mary McCarthy
George McGovern
Marshall McLuhan
Bess Myerson
Clifford Odets
George Orwell
Camilla Parker-Bowles
Ross Perot
Prince William
Marcel Proust
Gilda Radner
Nancy Reagan
Erich Maria Remarque

Diana Rigg
Geraldo Rivera
Nelson Rockefeller
Ginger Rogers
Linda Ronstadt
Jean-Jacques Rousseau
Françoise Sagan
Antoine de Saint-Exupéry
George Sand
Carly Simon
Neil Simon
Jessica Simpson
Jimmy Smits
Sylvester Stallone
Barbara Stanwyck
Ringo Starr
Isaac Stern
Patrick Stewart
Irving Stone
Meryl Streep
Donald Sutherland
William Makepeace Thackeray
Twyla Tharp
Henry David Thoreau
Mike Tyson
Abigail Van Buren
James Whistler
E. B. White
Billy Wilder
Robin Williams
Andrew Wyeth

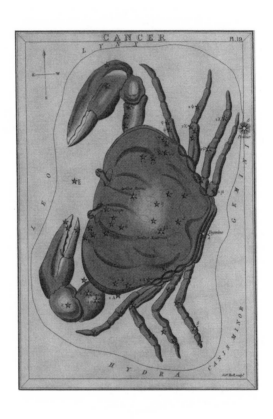

PART TWO

ALL ABOUT YOUR SIGN OF CANCER

CANCER'S ASTROLOGICAL AFFINITIES, LINKS, AND LORE

SYMBOL: The Crab

The Crab possesses an impenetrable exterior covering soft flesh underneath. At the first sign of danger, it withdraws into its shell and scuttles back to the sea, where it feels safe. The Crab has always been associated with the Moon (Cancer's ruler). In nature the Crab's growth is affected by the lunar cycles, and the Crab appears at the edge of the sea as the tides turn.

RULING PLANET: The Moon ☾

The Moon is Earth's one satellite, which waxes and wanes and exerts a powerful magnetic influence. In astrology, the Moon governs emotions and intuitive behavior, imagination, memory, and the unconscious. The Moon represents childhood and the past, and the accumulation of knowledge through the five senses (sight, hearing, taste, smell, and touch). From ancient times, the Moon has symbolized the feminine principle, and has been worshipped as a goddess (e.g., the Greek goddess Isis, the Roman goddess Diana).

DOMINANT KEYWORD

I FEEL

GLYPH ♋

The pictograph represents the claws of the Crab. It is also a picture of the human breasts (a part of the anatomy that Cancer rules). In symbolic terms, the glyph is two circles of the Sun connected to two crescent moons. The moons represent Cancer's desire to store memories and possessions; the circles tied to the moons represent force and energy expressed through emotions and imagination.

PART OF THE BODY RULED BY CANCER:
The Breasts and Stomach

Cancerians love to eat and have to fight weight gain in later years. They are also subject to digestive ailments caused by tension and emotional stress.

LUCKY DAY: Monday (Moon Day)

The day named for the Moon, ruler of Cancer.

LUCKY NUMBERS: 3 and 7

Numerologically, 3 is the number of imagination, expressiveness, and an open heart—and 7 is linked to thinking, knowledge, intuitive understanding, and inner wisdom. These qualities align with the nature of Cancer.

TAROT CARD: The Chariot

The card in the Tarot linked to Cancer is the Chariot. Ancient names for this card are the Powers of the Waters and the Triumph of Light. In the Tarot, this card represents the journey through life. The Chariot denotes creating a foundation and embarking on the new. It symbolizes triumphing over difficulties and finding emotional fulfillment. When this card turns up in a Tarot reading, it says a seed has been planted at the right time (the right phase of the Moon), and your enterprise will flourish.

The card itself pictures a princely figure riding in a chariot that has a canopy of stars. The chariot is drawn by two sphinxes, one black and one white. The prince represents the power of self, the chariot the powers of heaven and earth. The black sphinx symbolizes material desire and the white sphinx spiritual aspiration. Cancer must control both driving forces equally in order to arrive at a successful destination. The Chariot tells you, Cancer, that you have the power to overcome contradictory influences and strike out for the worthy goal. You are on a heroic journey.

MAGICAL BIRTHSTONE: The Pearl

Its luminescent luster is associated with the Moon (Cancer's ruler). Spiritually, the pearl represents acquiring emotional experiences. The pearl has always been linked to the feminine because of its softness, rarity, gentle sheen, and its origins in the sea. In many civilizations the pearl symbolized purity. Often worn to attract love, it was also used as a protective talisman against fire and lightning. For Cancer, the pearl is said to change bad luck into good and discord into harmony. It also brings to Cancer loyalty from a lover and support from influential people.

SPECIAL COLORS: Sea Green and Silver

The shimmering colors of the water and the Moon. Sea green also represents new life and fertility, and the color silver is imbued with connections to the archetypal goddess.

CONSTELLATION OF CANCER

The word *cancer* is Latin for Crab. In pre-Babylonian times (roughly the twenty-fourth to twenty-second centuries B.C.), the area of the sky in which this constellation of Cancer resides was associated with the Crab. Crabs walk sideways, then backward— the way the Sun appears to move as it arrives in Cancer, reaches the solstice, and then turns backward. This turning backward is a reminder of the turning of the tides of the seasons as the Sun begins its descending path. Egyptian mythology speaks of the Sun being pushed across the heavens by a celestial scarab beetle, and the Egyptians called the constellation of Cancer the Scarab.

CITIES

Venice, Amsterdam, New York, Algiers

COUNTRIES

Scotland, Holland, New Zealand

FLOWERS

Larkspur and Acanthus

TREES

Trees rich in sap

HERBS AND SPICES

Caraway, Verbena, and Saxifrage

METAL: Silver

The Latin word for silver means "white and shining." Since ancient times, the symbol for silver has been the crescent moon. Silver is inextricably linked to the concepts of water, reflection, illumination, and magic. For thousands of years this precious metal has been used in ornamentation and jewelry and in monetary systems. Silver is also used medically because it inhibits the growth of bacteria. The themes of the Moon, creative artistry, monetary value, and healing all relate to the sign of Cancer.

ANIMALS RULED BY CANCER

Those with shell coverings

DANGER

Cancer people are susceptible to accidents in the home. They are also prone to becoming victims of theft.

PERSONAL PROVERB

Great works are performed not by strength, but by perseverance.

Magnetic
Imaginative
Creative
Sympathetic
Intuitive
Compassionate
Great sense of humor
Romantic
High sex drive
Seeks emotional safety
Family oriented
Overprotective
Nostalgic
Sentimental
Tenacious
Retentive
Controlling
Hardworking
Fretful
Worrywart
Crabby
Moody
Complaining
Introspective

HOW ASTROLOGY SLICES AND DICES YOUR SIGN OF CANCER

DUALITY: Feminine

The twelve astrological signs are divided into two groups, *masculine* and *feminine*. Six are masculine and six are feminine; this is known as the sign's *duality*. A masculine sign is direct and energetic. A feminine sign is receptive and magnetic. These attributes were given to the signs about 2,500 years ago. Today modern astrologers avoid the sexism implicit in these distinctions. A masculine sign does not mean "positive and forceful" any more than a feminine sign means "negative and weak." In modern terminology, the masculine signs are defined as outer-directed and strong through action. The feminine signs, such as your sign of Cancer, are self-contained and strong through inner reserves.

TRIPLICITY (ELEMENT): Water

The twelve signs are also divided into groups of three signs. Each of these three-sign groups is called a *triplicity*, and each of these denotes an *element*. The elements are *Fire*, *Earth*, *Air*, and *Water*. In astrology, an element symbolizes a fundamental characterization of the sign.

The three *Fire* signs are Aries, Leo, and Sagittarius. Fire signs are active and enthusiastic.

The three *Earth* signs are Taurus, Virgo, and Capricorn. Earth signs are practical and stable.

The three *Air* signs are Gemini, Libra, and Aquarius. Air signs are intellectual and communicative.

The three *Water* signs are Cancer, Scorpio, and Pisces. Water signs are emotional and intuitive.

QUADRUPLICITY (QUALITY): Cardinal

The twelve signs are also divided into groups of four signs. Each of these four-sign groups is called a *quadruplicity*, and each of these denotes a *quality*. The qualities are *Cardinal*, *Fixed*, and *Mutable*. In astrology, the quality signifies the sign's interaction with the outside world.

Four signs are *Cardinal** signs. These are Aries, Cancer, Libra, and Capricorn. Cardinal signs are enterprising and outgoing. They are the initiators and leaders.

---

*When the Sun crosses the four cardinal points in the zodiac, we mark the beginning of each of our four seasons. Aries begins spring; your sign of Cancer begins summer; Libra begins fall; Capricorn begins winter.

Four signs are *Fixed*. These are Taurus, Leo, Scorpio, and Aquarius. Fixed signs are resistant to change. They hold on; they're perfectors and finishers, rather than originators.

Four signs are *Mutable*. These are Gemini, Virgo, Sagittarius, and Pisces. Mutable signs are flexible, versatile, and adaptable. They are able to adjust to differing circumstances.

Your sign of Cancer is a Feminine, Water, Cardinal sign—and no other sign in the zodiac is this exact combination. Your sign is a one-of-a-kind combination, and therefore you express the characteristics of your duality, element, and quality differently from any other sign.

For example, your sign is a *Feminine* sign, meaning you are receptive, caring, and resourceful. You're a *Water* sign, meaning you're creative, compassionate, deeply feeling, and intuitive. And you're a *Cardinal* sign, meaning you're an activist who can initiate new beginnings.

Now, the sign of Scorpio is also Feminine and Water, but unlike Cancer (which is Cardinal), Scorpio is Fixed. Like you, Scorpio is artistic and intuitive and has a rich inner life and an instinct for caring for others—but Scorpio is far more inflexible, fixed in its ideas and deeply invested in having control. Being the sign of depth, Scorpio's motivation is to explore what is hidden and concealed (hidden motivations, secret competitors), and thus keep itself safe. You, too, have an instinct for security, but you find safety in creating a family of relationships and collecting financial wherewithal. Fixed Scorpio is unyielding and immovable, whereas you, being Cardinal, are an initiator who's willing to move ahead. Your motivation is to form emotional bonds and express your artistic imagination.

Pisces, too, is Feminine and Water; but unlike Cancer (which is Cardinal), Pisces is Mutable. Like you, Pisces is nurturing and imaginative, drawn to the creative arts and to spiritual things. But Pisces, being Mutable, will vacillate, is indecisive and easily lured into side paths. Pisces is a dreamer who wants to escape harsh reality. Pisces is called a transcendent sign—it wants to transcend the confines of the practical and matter-of-fact and find joy in something more romantic and mystical. Pisces has vagueness in its thinking. It is willing to just let things happen and has neither your Cardinal ambition nor your concentration on getting the job done. You, too, are an imaginative dreamer, but you are a Cardinal sign and you want those dreams to come true. You are a focused *doer*.

POLARITY: Capricorn

The twelve signs are also divided into groups of two signs. Each of these two-sign groups is called a *polarity* (meaning "opposite"). Each sign in the zodiac has a polarity, which is its opposite sign in the other half of the zodiac. The two signs express opposite characteristics.

Cancer and Capricorn are a polarity. Cancer is the sign of home, childhood, family life, and creating a safe nest. You seek close personal relationships and are happiest surrounded by the familiar and those you love. You need emotional intimacy as well as emotional security. You have *simpatico* and understanding, and are the person most in touch with your feelings. In all aspects of your life, you want to express those feelings. Cancer is also the sign of "beginnings"—in the sense of creating and giving birth (to ideas, projects, offspring). Whether you're male or female, a "mothering" quality runs through your personality; you cultivate, care for, and attend to what you create.

As a Cancer, you're born with extraordinary sensitivity that throughout your life acts as your radar. You sense the emotional tenor in a room and feel what others are feeling. You pick up on what's not being spoken in the words someone is saying to you. Your radar is useful in business, too, for you get intuitive flashes of coming trends in public taste.

A difficulty is that your sensitivity also causes you to suffer. You're vulnerable, easily wounded, and hyper-attuned to others' behavior toward you. Flippant comments with a negative twist strike to your heart and serious criticism is often devastating. Being deeply feeling makes you capable of being deeply hurt.

Capricorn, your opposite sign, is the sign of reputation, career, and public standing. Cancer focuses on the inner world but Capricorn represents the outer world. Capricorn is goal-oriented, pragmatic, and ambitious, concerned with the image it projects. Natives of Capricorn search for power and fulfillment in the larger community. The motivation of Capricorn the Goat is to climb to the heights; it's an achiever. Whereas Cancer is impacted *by* others, Capricorn makes an impact *on* others. It has the strength to deflect the slings and arrows. Capricorn takes command; it is the authority.

Astrologically, you as a Cancerian can strengthen yourself by incorporating some of Capricorn's drive and practicality. Instead of struggling to make others happy and being hard on yourself, you can adopt Capricorn's concentration on doing what works and brings results, and not get bogged down in the sadness and defeat others lay on you. Cancer tries to take care of others whereas Capricorn tries to take care of itself.

Another lesson to learn from Capricorn is how to handle fear. Despite what Capricorn may be feeling, when facing crises of confidence it relies on discipline to keep on going. If nothing else, the act itself of pushing ahead step-by-step engenders certainty. A psychological truth is that action dissolves anxiety, and Capricorn always takes action. Both you and Capricorn are tenacious, but much of Cancer's tenacity has to do with holding on out of fear of letting go, whereas Capricorn hangs in to get the job done. Capricorn isn't the type to get lost in hopeless attachments.

In turn, Capricorn needs to open its heart the way you do. Capricorn cannot form relationships as easily as you do and often leads a lonely, cut-off life. If Capricorn could discover the joy that your generous spirit brings, it would never go back to its isolating ways. You, Cancer, know the true riches of intimacy.